ISBN: 9781314479461

Published by:
HardPress Publishing
8345 NW 66TH ST #2561
MIAMI FL 33166-2626

Email: info@hardpress.net
Web: http://www.hardpress.net

Elise A. Drexler

Woodside, Cal.

THY SON LIVETH

THY SON LIVETH

MESSAGES FROM A SOLDIER
TO HIS MOTHER

BOSTON
LITTLE, BROWN, AND COMPANY
1920

Copyright, 1918,
By Little, Brown, and Company.

All rights reserved

Norwood Press
Set up and electrotyped by J. S. Cushing Co., Norwood, Mass., U.S.A.

FOREWORD

In issuing anonymously a book of this character the publishers feel that a few words of explanation are necessary. The manuscript was received from an author known to them, accompanied by the following letter:

"The notes for this manuscript came into my possession several months ago, but I have not seen my way clear to submit it for publication until now, when the poignant grief of the world moves every heart to offer all it may of comfort.

"I am convinced that the simply presented letters of the soldier killed in Flanders contain comfort for all who now mourn or must mourn in the future. I should like to see these letters given a wide circulation through the medium of an inexpensive book."

Convinced of the sincerity of the author, and realizing that these messages from an American soldier were no ordinary spirit communications the publishers asked for further information. The author replied:

"I ask you to regard the book as truth,

unaccompanied by proofs of any sort, making its own explanation and appeal."

This book is published with the hope that it will fulfill the author's wish—give comfort to those of whom the war has demanded the bodies of their loved ones. Its message, as expressed in one of Bob's communications to his mother, is "There is no death. Life goes on without hindrance or handicap. The one thing that troubles the men who come here is the fact that the ones that loved them are in agony."

THY SON LIVETH

EVERY evening when I am at home, — and I am staying at home rather closely these days, knitting interminable skeins of gray yarn into socks for the boys in the trenches, — I go up into Bob's room and browse around among his traps and finger his tobacco-smelling clothes in the foolish way of mothers.

A man's room is a queer place — when the man has gone. This one, across the hall from mine, is the one Bob chose for himself when he was graduated from the nursery. It was not his first choice. With the announcement that he no longer wanted to be watched over at night, he selected and preëmpted the guest chamber in the farthest part of the house and moved in with his dog and a guinea pig. He put in the night there, too, without a whimper. But in the morning he informed me that he felt he ought to be near me in case I needed his help. He moved: and the room is one volume of his history from the day he was five years old. A record of his progress from that time until the bugles called him away. His books in the shelves range from Mother Goose Tales to Kant and his clan of thinkers, and up to what Morse planted and Marconi made to blossom. The last named are the thumbed books. Bob took to telegraphy as a spark takes to the air wave. He was one of the first to raise a wireless mast from the top of his home and, of course, I had to study and experiment with him. He bullied me into learning the code and being the party of the second part to take his messages. Looking back upon this now, I am impressed with the methods that are used by the Destiny that shapes our ends. Had it not been for that inkling of the science of telegraphy which I gained in our play I should not have heard a message that — but of this I will speak further.

It was something of a bore to me to put in my time trying to master a complex thing like the wireless; and, of course, I never did become proficient. But when the grind was over, and we both had acquired some speed and receptiveness, it was great fun; and we had a secret between us that made us pals. We used to sit up here in this room and pick up diplomatic secrets which we could not, fortunately, decode, and international messages which we could not, unfortunately, I believe now, decipher. And when Bob began to really grapple with the mathematics which were to make his path straight to his eagerly adopted profession of electrical engineering, he spent his leisure hours in trying to simplify Marconi's already simple apparatus.

We were here together the day Milly, the maid, brought up the afternoon mail and gave Bob a long, official-looking envelope which proved to contain an order from Washington to immediately dismantle the wireless apparatus. We had heard that amateurs were making nuisances of themselves — even in space; but it came as a shock to find that we were included in that list. Bob was literally a young thunder-god when he stood above his instrument and flashed his protests to the capital. Every time I glance toward that corner of the room I recall how he looked with his "mad on", as little Myra Kelly used to say. He is a good-looking boy, tall, athletic, strong-featured and blue-eyed, with his dark hair brushed straight back in the fashion young New York has so generally adopted. He had on his working togs at the time of which I speak: gray trousers, low collar and soft tie. He was tense with indignation.

I suggested that there might be something doing which we did not understand. He said he ought to be told why he was being bossed about like that; and he intended to find out what the deuce the government meant by it. We did not find out very much. But the curt message to dismantle without delay was not long coming. Bob showed a little fight. I told him that we had never been obliged to practice obedience to those in authority, so it came hard; but as Americans, united for the good of all in a common cause, it seemed the thing to conform to any requirement and ask why afterwards.

He did not yield without a struggle; but he yielded.

"It's a darn shame," he grumbled, as he came back through the window with the multiple antennæ in his arms and subdued the wires to a coil upon the table. "I believe I was just on the verge of hitting a plan to do away with a lot of this trumpery."

He sat on the edge of the table and dangled his long legs restlessly.

"Darn it," he repeated, in vexation, "I'm going to hire a little etheric wave of my own.

Why, mother, James" (he meant William James, of Harvard; rather a lion in his estimation) "James says that all the means of inter-mind communication are at hand and available. Their utilization only awaits developed human intelligence."

He started to put away the coils and various parts that he had brought in; but decided to leave the receiver where it was until he figured out some plan to make laboratory use of it. I left him fuming, literally, in a blue haze, and went down for tea.

Our house is one of the old homes on the Hudson below Tarrytown. I was born, married and widowed here: and here Bob first saw the earth-light. The people who live with us and serve us are, in turn, served by us. We feel ourselves, truly, a part of the soil. We live simply, and have had just the ordinary experiences of the comfortable American family in church and society and home. I want to dwell upon this sane and altogether unimaginative existence on account of what I have to tell later.

Milly had brought in the tea cart, and Bob came down to join me. He was still irritated; but he ate a whole jar of Damson jam and demolished the bread plate until

I had to remind him that we were only two hours from dinner.

"Let's go out somewhere," he jumped up, laughing. "Tramp or row, which shall it be? I'll get your wrap and scarf."

I chose the river. I knew the canoe would keep him occupied, and I felt that his nerves needed steadying. We went out and down to where the little boat was bumping its nose against the pier, and in a few minutes Bob was sending it, with his college stroke, toward the fleet that lay in the river. We have liked to be together in great moments — the boy and I. This was a great moment. We paddled in and among the ships and looked up at them with pride in our hearts.

"They look invincible, don't they?" I quavered.

He gave me a quick look.

"Mother, that's what you said the day we went over the *Lusitania*."

My heart plunged, sickeningly. The light seemed wiped from the sky. Bob was still staring as though he, too, had suddenly seen an object, long unheeded, before his eyes.

"What I want to know," he jerked out, "is this: Why aren't we at war with Germany, when Germany is at war with us?"

He stopped to shout to me not to rock the boat. I think I nearly sent it to the bottom of the stream. For, suddenly, I saw what had stopped our play with the wireless. All the events of the past few weeks, which had appeared of little consequence, loomed big before me.

"Let's go home," I said weakly. "And don't talk to me. Our country is at war — and I did not know it until this minute."

He devoted all his attention to getting free of the ships and avoiding the big swell made by a small tug. I wondered if it was the fading light that changed his face so when he said, at last: "You know what that means, mother?"

And I answered, untruthfully: "I know what it means."

He suddenly smiled and threw a paddle full of spray over me as we landed.

"Oh, you Spartan mother!" he laughed. "That 'come back with your shield or upon it' business does not go with such a fat little rascal-ma as you are. Come, I'll race you to the house."

But I held back.

"Robert, don't," I whimpered. "I am an old woman with a boy that is going to the guns."

He came back and put his arm around me, for I was trembling.

"We can't start the thing ourselves," he said; "we've got to wait for Washington. So cheer up. Who can tell what may happen to stave it off?"

But I knew that it was to be. Knew as well as I did months later when war was declared.

Meanwhile we went about our ordinary ways, with the exception that I concentrated on Red Cross and foreign relief work and withdrew from some of my club activities. Bob entered Columbia and came out for the week-ends, at which time I had our usual house parties which included so many pretty girls that he could not, for the life of him, fall in love with any one. People thought that I wanted to monopolize my son and keep him from his own love and happiness. But he knew that my hands were off his life. I was just an old campaigner showing a good way but leaving the youngster free to discover a better one, if he could. I was rather surprised, however, as the weeks passed and he was still heart free. I think his mind was more or less occupied with his electrical experiments and he still fussed over his demolished wireless station and spent many hours, when he should have been skylarking, over the instrument on the table yonder.

"Thunderation, mother," he said. "I can't get away from the feeling that I ought to get up to the nth degree in this science! The Germans are using it in ways that we do not know. And if I am called to fight, as of course I shall be, I want a trick up my sleeve that will beat the enemy at his own game. Anybody but you would laugh to hear me say it; but I have a hunch that I am going to be needed in some particular capacity before we win this war. And you mark my words: some day when you are up here in this old room of mine, you are going to hear from your little Robbie! I am going to put the thing together as well as I can and keep within the restrictions, and when I am in France I'll see if I can't figure out a system of relays or something or other so that I can get in touch with you."

I did not think it possible then. But I remembered what he had said when the old house was only a lonely, gray pile of empty rooms, and he had gone, with the unit, at the first call to arms.

What I felt to see my only son go to war is just what other mothers have felt and will feel as more and more young men are given to their country. But what further I have to reveal is what every father and mother should know. And quite simply I am going to tell it.

Bob was assigned to an Engineers' Corps and soon won his commission as second lieutenant. He was among the first to cross. I had a dozen letters from "Somewhere in France", and it was not hard to catch something of his spirit and enthusiasm. He was glorying in his hard work and his prospects for getting a whack at the Hun. He had qualified for wireless work, much to his delight, and had been out on a reconnaissance. Pershing, himself, had commended him. He warned me not to worry if I did not often hear — that letters are hard to get through. And now came one telling me of fun in camp and the brighter side of soldiering. He added that I had been a brick to him and made him a man.

I brought this letter up to read in his room and was laughing and crying over it, as women will, when the wireless signaled "attention." I sprang to the key, and in a moment I had the message that Bob had promised to find means to send me here. It is before me now as I made the translation from the Morse code, adding only the marks of punctuation:

"Mother, be game. I am alive and loving you. But my body is with thousands of other mothers' boys near Lens. Get this fact to others if you can. It's awful for us when you grieve, and we can't get in touch with you to tell you we are all right. This is a clumsy way. I'll figure out something easier. I'm confused yet. Bob."

So the news that my son had been killed came to me from his own intelligence by the methods we had used together in our experiments here in this very room. And so I am transcribing it, as he told me to do, for all to see who can be convinced of its sincerity. I have no explanations or proofs other than those that are given here: *A man who was killed in battle and is yet alive, and able to communicate with the one closest to him in sympathy, must make his own arguments. I have no knowledge of established psychic laws or limitations. But I know what I know.*

My own emotions, the more or less eventful chapters of my life and the lives of those about me, have nothing to do with this book of letters from far places. Bob and I want to ease, so far as may be, the intolerable anguish of the world. There was nothing spectacular or notable in his death. A month later the papers gave his name among hundreds of others that were mowed down by German guns. He must have communicated with me very soon after he fell. And first and last his urgent desire was, and is, to reassure and comfort the families of "departed" soldiers. In the messages that follow in their order, many will find a naturalness that must appear absurd. They will feel that, as in the case of all experiments beyond the bourne of the material senses, the spiritual communications are sadly mixed with earth. In this view I can sympathize. I have always turned away from books of alleged spiritual sources because I have felt that the author-soul was not advanced intellectually beyond the very ordinary human scale. I wanted the evidence of an immediate angelhood: all-wise, all-seeing, all-knowing. But I am now convinced that the processes of education among the worlds are somewhat the same; and I am decidedly comforted to realize that Bob Bennett is Bob Bennett still. Loving and slangy and familiar — but with a tremendously enlarged sphere of activities and absolute freedom from physical handicaps and the restricted period of years.

I have had, up to the time that I began to arrange for publishing, almost daily communications from my son. Some of these are personal letters which I shall not include in this work, lest in the future some one may pierce our necessary anonymity. But all those that seem to me to clear somewhat the mystery, and to simplify the methods of mental intercourse, are given as received. As will be noted by an early letter, the use of the wireless telegraph was soon abandoned for the better-known automatic writing simply as a matter of convenience. This will, of course, make skeptics say that these are the writer's subconscious emanations — nothing more or less.

Well, maybe they are. I cannot say that they are not. For I do not know what subconsciousness is. What stuff it is made of. Whence it comes or whither it goes. Maybe it is the bridge, the link between the mortal and immortal part of man. Maybe it is the inherent life which all scientists, from first to last, have sought without finding; that invisible stumbling block over which every well-built theory of atoms and electrons takes its headlong fall. If subconsciousness is one of these, it is more than probable that my boy is using its avenues of communication. For they must be clear enough from his end of the road. In fact, as will be seen in the notes, *if we were not asleep at our switchboards, we might all be in communication as easy and voluntary as are the people in the commonplaces who send telegrams to each other every day.*

Bob dwells upon the simplicity of it. He makes it plain — to me — that there is no need of the outside "hocus-pocus" of mystery-trumpery and cabinets and ignorant go-betweens, trances and crystal gazings, and all that sort of thing. He dwells on the discovery that the mortal really puts on immortality. He finds it difficult to describe what the difference is in what we call the spiritual world: the ways of living, eating, drinking, and dressing. "As far as I can see," he says, in one of his very late letters, "this is a place where one can carry out his own inclinations: for instance, I am plugging away at the wireless as I wanted to do before I came. I live with a lot of other fellows in camp just now."

In looking over his letters I cannot see that he has revealed the secrets of his new surroundings. He does not seem to be withholding anything purposely; but my curiosity in regard to who's who in Heaven and my questions concerning theological matters do not, as yet, receive attention. It may be that the Higher Diplomacy withholds these things, or it may be that we are not sufficiently enlightened to understand even these things with which we are continually confronted. I do not in the least understand the simplest phenomena of visible nature, but if Bob does not tell me how he gets his clothes, or intimate as to who does the work in the far places, I think there must be something apocryphal about his messages. And because of unbelief I fall back into the common attitude: a woman mourning for her son and cannot be comforted.

Faith has accomplished about every duty assigned to it, apparently, but the recognition of the free progress of the liberated soul. "Proof, proof," we call. But there is no proof. And so some saturnine man builds a creed out of his own meager understanding. And he puts heaven high and hell low, and a weak and violent God between them. If I had not the certainty that these communications I have are authentic, the literal messages from my son to me, I should still rather accept a pleasant faith on trust than an unpleasant one on the same condition.

One thing alone is certain,—the inevitableness of that change which most of us call "death" and poet-seers, like Wordsworth, call "transition." The words are synonyms. My boy has brought me to a sense of the sane and simple naturalness with which our family life goes on when we have finished this classroom work and progressed to far places. I think there are analogies in nature at every hand: millions of little shelled creatures, the names of which I do not know, and as many more minute organisms undergo successive changes and developments that are not less marvelous than the emergence of the soul from the body.

Those who have experienced death have found it easy: particularly those who have gone out in the crash of battle or tremendous and sudden disasters. Bob speaks at first hand of this. And from now on his letters must bear the consolation that he so wishes to extend: Blessed are they that mourn, for they shall be comforted.

Letter Number 2 (by wireless)

Attention: Get this across — there is no horror in death. I was one minute in the thick of things, with my company, and the next minute Lieutenant Wells touched my arm and said: "Our command has crossed: Let's go." I thought he meant the river, and followed him under the crossfire barrage the Tommies made, up to a hillside that I had not noticed before: a clean spot not blackened by the guns. Lots of fellows I knew were there, and strange troops. But they looked queer: I glanced down at myself. I was olive drab all right. But my uniform was not khaki: it seemed to be a fabric of some more tenuous kind. I had no gun. I overtook Wells. "What in the deuce is the matter with me, with us all?" I asked. He said, "Bob, we're dead." I didn't believe it at first. I felt all right. But the men were moving, and I fell in line. When we marched through the German barbed-wire barricades and in front of the howitzers, I realized that the body that could be hurt had been shed on the red field. Then I thought of you. Sent that wireless from an enemy station in the field. The officer in charge couldn't have seen me. But he heard, I guess, by the way his eyes popped. He sent a few shots in my direction, anyway. I am using an abandoned apparatus in a trench to-day, depending on relays. We are assigned to duty here for the present, according to Wells. I don't know how he knows. It seems while we have no supernatural power to divert or stop bullets, we can comfort and reassure those who are about to join us. There has been much talk about the presence of one supposed to be the Savior among the dying. I should not wonder if that were true. The capacity for believing is enlarged by experience. But as yet I have no more real knowledge than any of the other fellows. I will let you know as I gain information. Others, like me, will pick up and relay the messages.

Number Three (by wireless)

Attention: As I see this war, a curious understanding of its purpose and ultimate result is dawning in my mind. The soldiers are the pick of humanity. The young, brave, blameless manhood that has been brought to its majority on the earth so that it may form an ideal democracy in this existence which, I am told, is of permanent character. I am bungling the big idea. But, you know what I mean, mother. I'll grow clearer, maybe. Wells is getting to be a whale of an oracle. Some of the fellows are in a funk, and others are sullen and unhappy: homesick, I guess. The young married men mostly. If they could get in touch with their folks, it would be all right. That's why I want to try and simplify some system of communication. You have never failed me: and now if you can get it firmly fixed in your mind that I am I, not what is vulgarly called a ghost but a being just as much as I ever was, we can start something worth while. It's got to begin with some one as level-headed as you are. I'm called away.

Letter Number 4 (by wireless)

Attention: We hit upon the key word, when we agreed to use the word Attention in our wireless practice. It is the word that unlocks the inner, or secret, ear to hear otherwise inaudible voices. Do you get me? I mean: when you want to talk with me, concentrate your mind by calling your own faculties, the unused ones, mostly, to "attention." See if they don't respond. It may require practice, but I am told there is no reason in the worlds, — notice the plural, — why we should not talk with the greatest ease and without any mechanics. Come up and try to-morrow. See if I can't project my thought direct to yours. Bring pencil and tablet if you want to. But a fellow here who knows all about automatic writing says there is no pencil-guiding by unseen hands about it. The recipient just takes dictation. Better bring the pencil. You will want to report this just as it is for our purpose. I'll find out all I can, but just now we are engaged here in relief work. Some of the chaps are very young, and we see them through. I'll explain about those unused faculties when I learn more definitely about them.

Ed. note. I tried to write automatically that afternoon but what I got did not satisfy me. I seemed to be "faking" the message. I gave it up and called Bob by wireless as I used to call him. He did not answer. I tried again with the pencil and had a few words. But afterwards we progressed with increasing ease and freedom by means of that method. The unnumbered messages following were all automatically written.

This is harder — will have to practice. But it can be done.

Try to realize that thought is the one thing that is absolutely unlimited. You can send your thought to the most remote place as easily as you can direct it to something in your immediate neighborhood. Science has not explained why. Inter-space communication is not more mysterious than this. I want to put this over, mother. Not on our account alone. But because the little old world needs comforting. If we can convince folks that this is true, we can go a long ways toward wiping out sorrow. I must go.

Don't go to mediums. Some are, of course, genuine. But the dollar sign is apt to cover fraud. If you want to get in touch with us — get in touch. That is, get into a quiet corner and listen with your inner ear. Your unused finer perceptions. You will be able to really hear what I am saying, after some practice. I am told this by a man who has come to instruct us. I think, on my own hook, that you will have to rid your mind of worry or prejudice before we can make much headway. Any one who wants to can put out a mental wire that will be picked up. But you must "beware of strangers!" Quote that. There are scalawags ready to jump into all conversations and mix up things if they are permitted to do so. Keep your wires clear.

You ask how to keep the scalawags away — and who and what are they? I don't just know who they are. I'll try and find out. But you have to "make a law." That sounds occult and I do not want anything to be spooky or unnatural in these letters. But that is the expression I hear often concerning this particular difficulty. These wire tappers cannot get by, it seems, unless you permit them to fool you. You say: "I will not entertain mischievous spirits" — or something like that; and they beat it. I do not know why that is efficacious. But it is.

I have just come in from duty. I mean by coming in that I have come back to what I may describe as field headquarters. As I get more accustomed to conditions, I see that there are about a thousand men here, some of them boys from my regiment. We are really what might be called ambulance or Red Cross units, working to relieve suffering among the wounded and to guide newcomers. Mother, the soul leaves the body as a boy jumps out of a school door. That is, suddenly, and with joy. But there is a period of confusion when a fellow needs a friend. Quote that. We are the friends. I guess that is the best explanation I can give. I told you Jack Wells came through with me.

He has gone away now. I am told we go to other departments of usefulness, as others, suited to this field work, come on here. I will tell you as much as I can.

You complain that you cannot really get much of an idea of conditions here from what I tell you. I want you to be able to take my dictation like a prize-winner and, in the meantime, I'll try and get a line on things here. So far it is nothing very different from what we knew before the change. We go and come and serve. But evidently we are not seen. We do not seem to need food or sleep. I suppose we absorb moisture. I think our tenuous bodies are composed like clouds. But I do not know. Any way, your boy's heart is still in the right place.

I see your mind like a white screen, and I know I can write on it. Let's make a regular job of this book. You can edit the copy you get, of course. But don't put any literary frills in it, will you? When we get into the swing of it tell some of the other mothers. But teach them how to establish communication with their boys, themselves.

I guess you had better wait until you feel me calling you after this. We have important duties that we should not leave. About telling others. That is what we are doing this for, isn't it? A kind of a "comfort ye, my people" idea. But we must be very wise and level-headed. I don't believe I should try to get messages for others. Every man his own medium is the best plan. It would be human nature to doubt the genuineness of a letter from this side. Faith stops short at this threshold. But show some friends who need this particular kind of comfort what you know. Don't back out when you are laughed at. It's all in the big business we have taken on.

We do not know anything about the outcome of the war. Some of the teachers — a large number have now arrived and are mingling with us in a friendly way — refer to past calamities in which the race has been practically obliterated and the earth reformed and repopulated. From this point of view that is not such a terrible thing to contemplate. For we must start on the fact that the soul is immortal. There is no death for the individual. As so many — even material-minded men — realize, *the body is an exchangeable garment and does not count in the history of the man.* It seems that there have been an interminable number of races and nations lost in obscurity. They have moved on to other worlds, as this present race must be moved on. I do not know why civilization is allowed to reach a high mark before it is wiped off the slate. But that has been the rule, and so the Creator must have a purpose.

I asked one of the teachers, and he said that the earth is a preparatory planet. The human race is marked for an advanced existence and is brought to as high a degree of perfection as may be necessary to bring up the average. That is: The high degree of intelligence of the greater number lifts the lesser in the scale. We begin the new existence where we left off in the old. The more we have gained, the greater our advancement among far more favorable conditions. That is not clear. I'll get a better hold on the idea.

There are a number of dogs with us. I do not know whether they are astral dogs or not. They look just the same to me, and they go with us and help with our work.

The boys who come out are simply delighted to see them.

Jack Wells is back with us and in immediate command of our company. He has been to see his mother and he is one happy boy. She is somewhere here. Has been out for a long time. But one of the messengers found him for her and he got immediate leave to go. That sounded pretty good to me. He will tell me about things later. We are very busy.

Don't try to hold your pencil any differently than you hold it ordinarily, mother, dear. I am not guiding your pencil. As I figure it out, I am simply dictating these letters, by some improved form of telepathy, to your mind. You do the writing. It is wholly simple. I really talk, and you hear. Please get that to our audience. We all have perceptions and faculties that are capable of lifting us into supermen. The rub is we do not suspect our own powers. Do not let yourself be led into a maze of reasons why this thing cannot be. What is, is. If a theory of cosmic consciousness accounts for these communications to any one; if he thinks your mind is drawing them from a reservoir which holds dream stuff and the intangible echoes of the thought of all ages, let it go at that. Don't argue.

It is a funny thing that people always want to accept the most difficult creeds and to believe the most elusive doctrines. They (people) are a bundle of credulity and stubborn doubt. Of course their eyes will be opened in good time. But think what peace of mind they are missing. There are horses here, too. Good old fellows, that nose a chap's shoulder. I can't answer for them yet, or the dogs either!

I told you that we are not given any power over bullets. That we can comfort but not save from what you call death. That is not quite the case, I find. Jack Wells directed me to stand by a junior lieutenant to-day and impel him this way or that to avoid danger. In this way I discovered that my perceptions are much more sensitive than they were before I came out. I can estimate the speed and determine the course of shells. I stood by this fellow and nudged him here and there, kept him from being hurt. I asked Wells if that was an answer to prayer. Wells said, "No, the young chap is an inventor, and has a job ahead of him that's of importance to the world." An older man spoke up and said: "Prayers are answered. Don't make any mistake about that. But they are not answered according to material ways of looking at things." I did not get his explanation well enough to venture to repeat it. I'll know more, probably, as I go on.

Mother, dear, you are behaving like a brick. I tell you we are going to get this mortality play across the footlights. And it must be known as truth. I don't mean to call it that. But you know what is in my mind. If you could hear the cries that come to us from mothers and fathers and wives and orphans, you would know how continuously I plan and mull over this proposition. If you could just make them understand that *there is no death.* If you could just make them know that they can call their own loved ones to them and hear, at first hand, that all is well beyond what has truly been called "the veil." It is not more than that. It is not as much. A veil is woven fabric more or less resistant. We are separated from our living (I wrote living; please cross it out, because it would indicate that we are dead, and we are not) own folks by nothing but those unused faculties I spoke of on your side. *Urge immediate development of these faculties.* Teachers will, I am told, soon appear who are capable of waking these sleeping senses. With that accomplishment we shall be face to face.

I can't read your mind yet. Speak to me as you would if you could see my face. Fancy that we are sitting in the dark but fully aware of each other's presence. If you ever need me, especially, do not hesitate to call me, or at any other time. If I do not hear you, some one will carry the message on until I get it. I have been so engrossed with these strange happenings that I may have seemed cold. But dear, dear mother, I never loved you better than I do now. And I understand all the subtle wonders of your love for me, as your son, far better than I did before. I know you long for the touch of my hand, my big, red grip that you used to be too game to wince under. But be sure that I am Bob, your Bob, and that we are going to have all the time there is together.

You remember that we felt rather a shock when that woman you know edited a book of letters from this side in which clothes and victuals and drink were much dwelt upon. I think some one of those mischief-makers that I referred to some time ago was fooling her. There are, as I explained, many intelligences here that delight in playing jokes on the credulous when they can get on the etheric wave that is being used by communicants. Of course I am not competent to make any positive statement. But I think the conditions here are wholly spiritual. The physical body and its functions have been discharged. Only the emotions of the soul remain. I wonder if I can make that more plain? I surely want to be a reliable correspondent, and I want to show that while the human machine ceases with the body, all the fine raptures that made the happinesses of earth are with the spirit. I, myself, appear just as you last saw me. But I am doubtless clothed in that same cloudlike vapor that composes my body. I am the same, yet not the same, freed from the gross conditions that attend humanity and yet capable of love and the higher expressions of marriage. I shall have opportunities to learn definitely concerning these things and I will tell you — as frankly as I have always told you things that boys generally keep from their mothers.

I have not seen any one with wings. We cover any number of miles without fatigue. That is a good thing, for I have not heard of any rest from labor being advocated. We do, however, rest others. We ease the boys in the trenches — they wonder how they can sleep so comfortably on the hard, wet ground, — and for several nights, now, I have been holding a sick boy in my arms. These duties keep us occupied almost all the time, but we have undiminished force and are never weary. I hear continually of the presence of the Savior on the battle fields. I think this must be true. Anyway, the dying are certain that He has been with them, and they are happy. They speak of His love.

Tell this to mothers. Jack Wells talked with me last night, and he gave me a great description of what he saw when he went away for his visit. His mother heard that he had come west, and she sent a messenger for him. It seems the messengers are somewhat different from the rest of us. I will speak of that later. Jack accompanied this messenger. They pierced the envelope of the earth. Or at least found some exit. From what Jack gleaned, he thought the world we have believed to be so tremendously powerful is really much like the smallest ball in the nest of balls that are carved out of ivory by Orientals. One within the other, you know. You have to penetrate one to gain access to another of larger size. So, as I understand it, the spiritual worlds of our solar system are swung into space, not separately, but together, each on its own axis but all moving in harmony as one. The progress of the soul is through these spheres up to the highest development. The earth is the material or lowest form. We have often wondered why Christ came to save one little planet when He seemed to belong equally to the whole Universe. But it seems that this is the cradle of humanity. That herein was established the race of men, an independent order of creation that was to acquire through knowledge of sin and pain and sacrifice, a strength that should fit men for leadership among supermen. Jack's mother is in the next world, and from what he says I was not right about the manner of living. His mother received him in a home where other members of the family were waiting for him, and it was just a happy reunion. While he was conscious that they had all passed through the experience of death, he could not really see any change in their appearance. They were dressed in what appeared to be fabrics but were probably vapor stuff, and they seemed to eat and drink and live much as they lived on earth. It is said that business is conducted along ideal lines, and agriculture is brought to perfection. There are many chemists and inventors at work to develop resources, and as the different globes are intercommunicable, the earth gets the benefit of the discoveries. This figure is often used, and I guess it is a good one. Consider the system of planets all incorporated in a final atmospheric envelope as so many rooms in a school. All doors are open for the entrance and exit of every one, high or low, in the whole school: the separations are mental. A pupil can jump over any grade if he has the ability. Those who qualify on earth can enter advanced classes or conditions. The return or reincarnation of a spirit is a matter concerning which I am not informed. I know that many return many times. I do not as yet understand how this is accomplished, or whether it is voluntary or an arbitrary law. I hope I shall not have to go back. I'd rather take a fling among the other worlds. I could not be your boy; and I'd rather have you than any other mother.

Jack's mother and sister are teachers. It is the business of those who are familiar with the law of the place to instruct others. Ruth Wells was killed in an automobile accident a day or so before she was to have been married. Her lover went out with the Canadians and has been doing great work in the air. He came out (died) while Jack was there, and he came straight to Ruth with a messenger she had sent to watch for his arrival. Now they are incorporated in one form. I do not quite understand this yet. I shall have to see the married to know what that means. But I am told that a man and woman are really one. Each half of a whole. When they are mates they are united. The matter of plural marriages is settled in this way. The real mates are brought together. The others finding their complementary selves. It is a difficult subject. Better leave it out of the question until I get it in clearer shape. I do not know which side dominates this dual personality. I talked it over with a group of fellows here — those who have just come out — and none of us like the idea.

You ask where I am? I am right now in and about Verdun, and I have not often been away from my division. As I told you, some of us are assigned to escort duty. When the boys come west, — quote that, — we meet and guide them across the Invisible Line. Most of them feel perfectly fit when they come. But some few are confused or frightened. Particularly about the sorrow of those they leave behind. Try and make this point plain to the families. The boys are all right. Do not mourn for them. Every tear tortures the dead. Know that they are loving their folks and anticipating a meeting. I must go.

The most important thing for us to consider is this: We are just as much alive as we ever were, and the ties of love continue. This does not necessarily mean the ties of relationship. Love is the dominating force. For instance, the fact that I am your son, born of your body, is not the thing that will unite us in this advanced life. There is a subtler bond which has nothing to do with consanguinity. Spiritual affiliation or sympathy is about what that is, as well as I can make out.

But I am not yet far enough advanced to make any definite or authoritative statement. I only want to start this whole propaganda of comfort on the one sure thing: *There is no death.*

This is during a lull in a battle. I inquired of the teacher why the German soldiers are so devoted to the Kaiser, how blind belief of millions came to be fixed on this one weak madman. For he is a lunatic. It was explained that a Mesmeric wave has swept Germania from the throne to the far borders since William's grandfather ruled. Mesmer, the Austrian, set forces into operation then, which he has maintained since through the mind of the present Kaiser.

I do not know whether that is a fact of science or a personal opinion. The man who told me is a stranger to me. He may not have any real information.

Mother, I have found out another thing from this point of view. There is little or no fear of death among men who go into battle. The soul seems to remember, suddenly, that it may be about to repeat an interesting experience. The physical side of the soldier is dominated by the spiritual and carried on with a kind of thrilling joy. The meanest man sometimes surprises his comrades by exhibitions of courage. This is the reason. In this connection I must mention Cooper. You will remember that I wrote you about him when I enlisted: He seemed to be the one blot on our regimental 'scutcheon. A sniveling "willy boy" who was afraid to go home in the dark. We all wondered how he stood the examiner's gaff and was accepted. He had prayed, very likely, that he would be turned down. Well, he came west since I last wrote you. I happened to be near when the grenade fell in the trench and saw him grab it in his arms and scramble out with it before it exploded. He saved a whole company: among them many wounded. I went with him over the top and yelled, "Bully for you, Coop, old man!" Then the bomb blew away his mortality, and he saw me. We left the field together, and I took him back among the hills where the particular group of helpers headed by Jack Wells gave him the glad hand. He's all right and a trump among us. Get word to his mother.

I got your word about the difficulties you are meeting in conveying the information. Isn't it curious that the human mind instinctively rejects the easiest answer to a problem? Do you recall how we laughed over that epitaph on a little white gravestone in New England:

> "*Since so quickly I was done for,*
> *I wonder what I was begun for?*"

Well, get such comfort across as you can, but do not try to convince any one that you communicate with me. You would probably be carted off to a padded cell if you should tell all we shall talk about. For I feel that we shall get on further soon. Wells says a new company is to relieve us, and we will "proceed to our destination."

Cooper is in a blue funk about his mother. She is frantic with grief, and he cannot communicate with her. She is like many Christians. She subscribes to a creed — but she doesn't believe it. If she would just take her pencil in her hand, and let Coop do the rest! Then she would come to know that her son and all the other sons are living and only kept from being happy and full of new and splendid ambitions by the tears of those they love on earth. To mourn is natural: but it really isn't natural to be hopeless.

I got that little hint you wired me about knocking Christians. You see I still need your bully judgment. I remember your little old tenet that no cause is won by criticism. And I believe we have a cause, mother. Of course this matter of automatic writing, as you call it, is old and generally discredited. Some big, independent thinkers know that it is genuine in the main. But most folks are from Missouri. You have to show them something that can't be shown to material senses before they consent to be comforted. Too bad, isn't it?

If you could see the way the fellows here feel, you would know why I harp on publicity for this scheme of communication. There may be a better one. But I don't know about it yet. Get two or three of the sanest women you know who have lost dear ones, — and almost every one has or will, — and persuade them to try. Show them how you do. Tell them there is no mystery or flubdub. Tackle Mrs. K., she is level-headed. Take her fully into your confidence — show her these letters if you want to. Tell her to spread the truth. You know how you feel when you have been cross or unjust, or something like that, to some one you really care for. You can hardly wait to make up. That's the trouble on both sides with those who cross the line and those left there. Grief is mostly remorse for things done or left undone, and there is no chance to make up. Coop says he was a rotter to his mother, and he has lately heard her crying that she had been harsh with him when he was a little boy. How quickly they could square things if she only knew that he was closer to her in actual presence and in sympathy than he had ever been before.

I want to speak about the little things that rankle in your heart. You remember when you spanked me with the hair-brush: and a thousand wasps of memory sting you. Let's laugh! Just as we should if we recalled them together when you could see me grin. What matters now — and always — is that understanding love that binds us. We have the particular thing that will bring us face to face again! We are mother and son. But we are more than that. We are pals. That is what counts. I have been told this by an instructor from Somewhere in Space. You see we are still right near you in the envelope of the earth, assigned to the battle fields for service to the wounded and the dead. Quote "dead." It is a misapplied word. But just as French officers are being sent to the American cantonments to teach advanced methods of fighting to our troops, so experienced teachers on this side are moving among us, getting us ready to meet and understand new conditions. They look like and they are men.

As far as I can make out, we are going to a very real world: a globe divided into parts of land and water: one of the near stars, maybe. I'll find out about that. We are, I am informed, much the same as we were before we came; except that we are no longer limited or hampered by the flesh and bone body we formerly occupied. We have been "raised spiritual bodies" just like the old Book says. But it is the spirit that quickeneth, isn't it? So there you are. We are still folks — and not still folks either — nobody dumb here, as far as I can learn.

To return to the worlds. I hear that we are to swing along in the old reliable solar system with the rest of you. It seems Mother Earth has all the time been wearing her right title. I have heard that the earth is the cradle, or the incubator, of the human race, and that the other planets, all intercommunicable, are inhabited by those who have passed through the earth experience. There may be other Mother planets. I don't know. But "His kingdom ruleth over all."

I have not tried to write you lately, because I have been on the job night and day. The world we are to go to will be the Country of the Young in fact. So many boys are coming out. And they are all right. Do get that word across. Do make it your business to get that across. *The one thing that troubles the men who come here is the fact that the ones that love them are in agony.* Get around on that side of the question with your old pluck and tell the mothers and fathers and sisters and wives to stop crying. No man can stand the sight of tears, the sound of sobs. They feel it much worse here, because they can't get in touch to comfort. It's awful. It will seem queer when I say that we don't bother much about any physical pain our folks suffer. That is a transitory thing. We know it for what it is. But we are still capable of mental anguish. That is the hell-material. And every tear shed on earth falls on a heart here. A wail is continually coming to us from every side. Have them stop it.

I know you can't do much toward spreading this truth. But do something. What do you care what the neighbors think? If a few really get in touch with us the news will spread. Tell them there is nothing solemn and mysterious about it. Get a number of women together. I'll come and bring an operator. Did I explain? If you can't send messages yourself and some cannot now,—you transmit them just as we do when we drop into a Western Union or Postal and write out our night letters. You are a good receiver because we had all that wireless work together when I was a kid. Get the women: not the highbrows who know too much to believe anything as natural as inter-space communication. But simple, homey mothers. I was wrong about Mrs. K. Too much learning has made her mad. Think of some one simpler, more convincible.

Make it plain that this communication is given from my mind to yours as plainly as an old man at 26 Broadway talks to his secretary about other invisible riches. Better not say that. What I want to do is to rid this system of all its bewildering and mystic features. Make an engagement for me: I'll attend, mentally; then sit down and take my messages openly, before folks. Every one fears the unknown and minimizes the commonplace.

The limitations of the human vision and the circumscribed range of the human perception of sound are what separate us. Not that we are forever, even in thought, hovering around our folks on earth. That would be rather horrid, wouldn't it? We observe proprieties and wait for invitations. Just while we are trying to establish communications, we are making frequent calls. After that we go about our business and send our messages by operators from wherever we may be — and we'll make visits as boys go home at Christmas or birthdays. If you send very urgent calls, we must answer. But you will not do this when you know that we have important work to do in our environment. I do not know as yet what it is to be in my case. It may be electrical engineering or some wireless telegraph development. I hope it may be something that will lead to an understanding between the worlds.

You ask who else are here beside the soldiers. In this particular group are only the men and women assigned to field service. Mostly soldiers and Red Cross nurses. But we have encountered many women on the battleground and among the wounded. These are mothers and wives who are on this side, and they look after their own. I am told that the war has called all these spiritual forces into action. There is a mobilization here of the generation immediately connected with the troops, — fathers and mothers and near of kin, — to attend these boys and to bring them out.

We are still in the earth envelopment. Jack Wells says we may be transferred to America. I would give anything for a little fore knowledge now. But we have not progressed far enough to claim that. Of course our intuitions are sharper than they were before we came out. That is about all. And we all think that America is covered by a net of German treachery and an unthought-of danger from within. There are cunning devils, in the flesh and out of it, conspiring against the United States. This young giant-land of ours must not be beaten. The final victory must be with our flag. Let the women stand by. Beg them to do as you are doing. Yes, I know. Have them sell their jewelry and pour every luxury into the war fund. I'll tell you all I learn from time to time.

A fellow of the —— Marine Corps has just come to this rest station with a girl. He is dazed and does not seem to recognize her. She is a schoolmate of his, and very likely has kept a little romance folded away in her soul. I hope he will recall her when he gets his bearings. She has been on this side for several years. Seeing her around him makes me think I'd like to have a pretty little thing like that fluttering around me.

Mother, dear, when you are writing for me, be rather careful not to interpolate. You do not, much. But we want this to be pretty direct, don't we? Our only object now is to get this comfort,—this possibility of communication between the seen and unseen living, — to those that mourn. You do not feel any fatigue or strain, do you? Your arm does not get numb? Why should there be any effect of that sort? This is simply thought transference, dictation. A perfectly natural thing. Induce others to get into communication with these boys who want to butt in while I talk to you. I am besieged to give you addresses. But if you can get any publisher to take these notes, I guess that will be the best way to get an audience. Try —— or ——. They are both good firms and liberal thinkers.

I hope I can go on before long where I can get into working harness. I believe my mind is going to be clearer and quicker to act than formerly. I mean to work on devices to combat the German machines. If I succeed I'll get in touch with Edison, if he is still in the game there. In the meantime I'll attend to my job of easing the hurts made by the guns. We have been taught to do that; otherwise there would be great suffering. I must go now.

We are immediately going to start for the Outside. Other companies have come to take our places on the field. I am distinctly agitated. Do not know whether I shall be able to get in touch with you or not. Shall certainly try. Anyway, you will know that I am all right, and that some day we are going to be together again. Be a game little sport, and don't cry. I'll feel your tears if you do. And they will make me wretched. Everything is all right. No doubt, whatever. I hope that I shall be able to visit you. Anyway, we are mother and son and — pals, always.

I am still in the atmosphere. We had prepared to leave for a destination unnamed: for others arrived to take our places as helpers on the battle field. Some men, or I suppose they are angels, came to act as our escort. Jack Wells got our particular bunch — about forty — into shape, and we stood in marching formation on a little hill until the word was given to start. We did not fly or float or anything like that. We just marched at a good rattling pace. The only thing strange about it was that we did not mind such natural obstacles as forests or rivers, but went right along through or over them. This was the case out of doors. But we did not pass through closed buildings or walls. At all times we looked for the openings or gates. I asked the man (angel) about whether we had really bulk or weight. He answered me. But I didn't understand well enough to make it clear, I am afraid. I think he meant that our bodies are heavier, or denser, than air. As these facts are made known to me, I will tell you. We passed through several villages, one of which I had seen on the way to the line. It had been shelled and destroyed. There were human bodies everywhere. They looked like, and were, no more than so many abandoned shells or coverings. From this point of view there is no more in death than removal from one house to another. In most cases the separation of the soul and body was complete. Where there was still some clinging to the body on the part of the self, some of us waited to comfort and cheer. Now and then we came across a frightened or dazed spirit: and we helped there. But there were many men and women from this side present among the ruins, and their special care seemed to be the children. Some beings (angels) literally carry the little ones on their bosoms.

I had supposed that we would leave the atmosphere of the earth by ascending into higher regions. We are all more or less influenced by Raphael's "Ascension", I suppose. But it seems that there are points of egress reached by defined channels. Ports of departure. At present I cannot tell you where the one we were assigned to is located, because we were recalled. And the manner of the recalling will interest you. The march was well under way when there was an order to "right about face" and we started back. Jack Wells was marching with the Man in command, — I have not yet learned his name or what to call him, — when he turned around and said he had orders to return. How he got the orders puzzled me. There were no messengers or mechanical means like telephones or wireless. But it seems we acquire the ability to hear anything addressed to us, personally, through any amount of space. That is how you reach us. *And what we are trying to do now is to have you hear us as well as we hear you.* Please italicize this when you print what I say. I wish you would read Swedenborg again, and compare what he says with what I may be able to tell you. You remember we read a book of his together that winter I had to stay indoors. I hope to see some of our great forces over on this side, or beyond this particular side, as I progress.

Just when that will be I cannot guess. It seems we are still needed on the battle fields where our work is to ease the wounded. This we are able to do. Emphasize this, mother. For every boy that is hurt or terrified, there is a comforter. I wrote you that we hear, continually, that the Savior is often seen on the fields. I have not dared to look, sometimes, when I have felt, rather than seen, a strange soft light. I am not ready to look just now. But there is no doubt but that He moves among the soldiers. I am called away.

I get all your messages, mother. I can only answer a few questions. Partly because I am not yet sure of many things here and partly because there seems to be no means of communication concerning certain conditions. That is: when we get beyond the usual, we are beyond the common medium of language. The words we know are inadequate to express our revelations. Of course until we move on into the Big Places, we are really on almost the same footing as though I too were in the flesh. But when the Big Places are reached, I shall have more difficulty in conveying my information. At least, so I suppose. Now

I am to continue in the ether for a time anyway. Ought to pick up considerable news for you. If I dwell on things that seem the least important, perhaps it is because of this angle of vision. Now the all important matter to the boys here is to have their folks know that they are alive and well and filled with intense enthusiasm and ambition. Take up the Bible and read it with this that I am telling you in mind. I expect, as time goes on, I shall be able to describe scenes and customs to you, — after the manner of the observant traveler, — but now what you must learn is this: In this intermediate place which is neither wholly material nor wholly spiritual, we are busy and so happy, or would be if it were not for the sobs and tears of our folks. Please do not give way to sadness, mother. And for heaven's sake (this is literally for heaven's sake) beg the mourners to stop crying, and to cease wearing black clothes.

We have returned to our former quarters on a hill above Verdun. The fighting is continual, and there is much for us to do. Many are coming out. Charlie Spenser came wandering across the field in a dazed sort of way. He was glad to see me and did not dream that I had been changed. He is not reconciled to death because he is in love with a girl on earth. That seems to break up the philosophy. A man can leave every one else with resigned calmness but the one girl he loves. He is in great mental agony, and I am going to get one of our instructors to take him in hand.

The angel came into my tent and talked with Spenser. I have got to get what he said clear in my mind before I transmit it to you; the purport of it is simply this: Each created being is the half of another created being. When these two halves are brought together, it is marriage. There may be many *alliances* in a person's life. But only *one marriage.* That sounds like the affinity business we heard so much of at one time. But you would not think it sounded that way if you heard this angel explain it. I'll get down to his real meaning and write more.

This is it. There are no separations of those who belong together. Emphasize "belong." Spenser's girl will come to him here if she is his other half, and their marriage will be consummated in heaven. I asked the angel what if the girl should marry, and he surprised me by saying she probably would, certainly should do so. That she should fulfill the law of her being on earth by wife and motherhood. That accomplished, she will find her spiritual mate and the man who had been her husband on earth will find his own complementary self. It all sounded simple and rather familiar. I think you will not be shocked when you really consider that we are not dealing with the ephemeral life of the body but of the eternal verity, the soul. There are some things I want to ask the Man when I can screw my courage to the sticking point. Among them is whether one who has not been in love, as we say, on earth, can expect such an experience here. I will find out and let you know.

I get any thought, I suppose, that is directed to me. I cannot undertake to say how or why. In fact I am not informed as to these things. I do not know why any more than I knew, in class, why one ray of light was white and one was violet. I read what the scientists said, of course, and let it go at that. Their facts did not dent my understanding.

If ever I send another message to our old neighbors, after this is done, I am going to urge them to open their minds to many things. From this point of view I am pretty sure that however wild a proposition may appear to be, it is certain to contain an element of truth. If millions of dusty papers lost on the shelves of the Patent Office might be brought out, I have no doubt that old What's-his-name would find among them a fulcrum to fit his lever, so he could go about moving the earth. That reminds me that we must not stop pushing these facts over prejudices and difficulties. Get them boiled down to the utmost simplicity. To a sentence, if you can. Life is continuous and souls go marching on. That's the big truth. All other things can be added unto it. Many things I say are not authoritative. But this thing is. Look in the Bible, with these spectacles on, and see. As far as modes of living, habits of angels, philosophies and opinions, my reports are likely to be as accurate as the average traveler's in an unfamiliar country. But I'll correct any misstatement as I go on and learn more. Our main business, now, is to establish definite lines of communication.

The fighting has swung back to about the place where I fell. Think of me as doing a man's part still, right in the battle. We do not fight. We form the relief division and bring comfort and aid to the wounded. Many of the soldiers see us; that does not mean, always, that they are dying men. They seem to have supernormal vision. I do not like that word. But let it go.

I was easing a boy in my arms; but he was very young, and he wanted his mother. I could not comfort him. Some One beside me said: "I will take him." I could not look up. But I knew Who it was. Let mothers hear of this.

Please do not elaborate anything I tell you, dear. I must go. A whole battalion is coming out.

I have not met any relatives. You know we are still on earth. Some of the boys who have folks in far places get leave to go and see them. But I feel that my job is right here. Awhile ago I lifted up a wounded color-bearer, and together we kept the flag from touching the ground. That seemed to be his main idea. I held him until relief came and promised to wait in case he should come west. But he is to recover. A girl from the Red Cross hospital was working alone, plucky as any one, regardless of the fact that a counter-charge of glorious furies in horizon blue had cut her off from her friends. A shell struck her; and later she let me guide her into the Quiet. She looks like one of the McL—— girls. But she is dazed and can't tell her name. She'll be all right soon.

I cannot tell when it will end. When or how. No one but God knows what plan is being evolved from this chaos of worlds. Do not put any faith in prophecies except those in the Book. I mean the Bible. I am not guiding your hand. Can't you understand? My thoughts flow into your mind, and your thoughts flow into my mind. Get some figure — the movement of tides, maybe, to fix this truth. Back and forth, carrying and releasing, delivering to and acquiring from the shores.

We are getting on famously, and as we progress I think we shall discover even greater facilities for expression. I think communication would have been established and accepted as a perfectly natural thing if the human mind had not opposed so many obstacles. Humanity makes images to represent God, invents machinery to improve on His gift of perception, and refuses to credit voices and visions that are not man made. Better cut them (obstacles) out. Criticism does not land us anywhere.

I am so busy that I do not think of saying the loving things I know you long to hear. But I never loved you better than I do now. I know more about you, and about mothers everywhere.

The Red Cross girl that I brought across the line is not one of the McL——s. But she is pretty and jolly and a bear for work. She is constantly with us on the field. Her folks live in Wisconsin, but she says they will have to wait until they come here before they learn that it is well with her. They believe in the immortality of the soul. But proof of their belief scares them. Her name is Ann. Sometimes she hears her mother cry. Then it is hard for her.

Many women are here now. And their work is mostly among the babies and young slain. There are lots of these. The little chaps are very popular. A nursery has been built on a shady hill. We have the same sun and planets that light you.

Women and men work together in natural harmony. There are preferences and avoidances and some sweethearting. But for the most part the business in hand occupies all of us. I do not know how it will be as we go on further. This is a great receiving camp. It looks as though it had been chosen by engineers and established as a model cantonment. I am impressed with the system that does not intrude itself as system. Yes. We dress and undress. There is a general commissary who issues our clothes in military fashion. I do not know how they are originally obtained. At first the stuff felt different from the material of the uniform I shed in Flanders. But now I do not notice anything peculiar about it. Maybe I am used to it, and have forgotten the old.

I know you miss me, mother. And that you are very anxious to come on. But sit tight until you get the signal. Sit tight, do you hear me, dear? And warn all with whom you talk against suicide. I do not gather from what I hear that curses afflict any poor soul that makes that mistake. But the self-inflicted death disarranges and delays the plans that are being shaped for the individual. Every detail of life is worked out with a thoroughness only possible in spiritual geometry. A sudden break necessitates rebuilding the whole theory. It may require skill for you to tell what you have to tell and yet restrain broken-hearted ones from throwing themselves across the invisible line. Of course, they want to rejoin their darlings. But that will be later. No one is received here now except soldiers assigned to duty and men and women of the Red Cross and military, and those who come from the war zone with death.

A great thing has developed and it shows which way the winds of God begin to blow. I have been assigned to pick up wireless from the enemy lines and transmit it to the Allies. I've worked the clock around on this. Every chance has been given the Hun to fight a fair fight. Now, it seems, the angels are arming against him.

There is no curse attached to anything, as far as I can find out. Laws are finely adjusted, and their principles are immutable, in the main. But God can change laws, even His own. There is nothing in all the worlds to handicap the big race the soul makes for perfection. We, here, are in the very beginning of it. The girl, Ann, says the immensity of the work ahead would appall her mother more than the threat of hell. She is so tired. You and your kind do not really know that the world is full of toil-tired women. So tired that they hate the thought of heaven unless it means rest. After all it is not for us to map heaven. I do not know what or where it is, or if there is such a state. We just want to tell what we do know. And that is, Life is not snuffed out by war or any other calamity. The Hun cannot kill the soul of a woman or a tree or himself.

None of my statements about less important matters are to be taken as certainties unless I quote our instructors. They may not be infallible, but I presume they are. But this is our big fact: I am really, vitally alive. All others who have passed the change called death are alive and progressing toward fuller life. Harp on that string. Keep at it. Do not let your mind become discouraged or confused. Nothing that I can write you is of any importance compared to this. I am called away.

I know what you are up against. You are in for ridicule and the sort of publicity that is hardest to bear. But have at it. Get the word across. Don't fix up my notes much. Let them smash away as they come right off the bat. They are not only to comfort the people there, but to relieve the boys here. They worry like the deuce over their folks. Some few who know what we are doing are after me all the time to help them get in touch with their own. They make constant efforts to communicate.

Think of the situation this way: A child (for instance) is screaming and sobbing in the terrors of nightmare. His mother tries to waken him, to reassure him, and tell him that he is safe in her arms, against her breast, that all is right. But she cannot make him listen and understand. There you have it. It's the same thing, exactly. Wake them up, mother. Hush their sobs. The Everlasting arms are not failing. All is well. "If it were not so I would have told you."

Don't argue. We cannot convince any one against his will. Let him believe or deny. You are only a messenger. One accepts the heartease you offer, or he does not. Perhaps by the time this page is printed, the light-which-is-to-be will be shining on the earth. Undoubtedly the mystery that befogs us is likely to be soon lifted.

The work of the young girls on the battle field is a revelation. They are the same kind of girls that you used to have out for the week-ends: pretty and cultivated and all that. But they have gone through some sort of transformation while they are still in the flesh. That is, the little, tinkly garments of silliness have dropped away and left fine spirit. But the women at home are not doing enough. The sacrifice has got to be made. Every one will be stripped down to soul before this is all done. Don't talk of houses and jewels and servants and lands when men are rebuilding the foundations of the earth with their bare hands.

Yes. We sleep and waken refreshed. I'm told we shall require food as we go on.

Jack's father and mother live in a house and have food and water. I think we absorb water, mostly. But when we pass springs, I stoop to drink.

The instructor (angel) whom I told you about is getting Charlie Spenser into line. He has made it clear that there can be no permanent separation of two parts of a whole. It appears that every one is or will be married. The twain shall be one spirit. I judge from his statement that marriage is consummated here.

You wonder how we stand the cursings that we must hear? I am told that all such sounds are produced by the gasses of terror and are a part of the crashing and rending of tortured souls. I do not believe the Divine Intelligence regards these explosions. Of course we are punished for defiance of law. That goes on in all parts of the spiritual as well as the material worlds. But (and I want to go cautiously here because I am not sure that I have cinched the big idea) some of our worst old sins show up small in comparison with others that we have been rather proud of, and referred to as "faults." I can't say what they are. I suppose each fellow knows his own.

Too bad that you are not able to convince Cooper's mother that he is all right. He is more than all right. And he may serve to illustrate a point I indicated recently. You know how weak he used to be, and dissipated? Rather worthless and all that? Well, he is one of the most esteemed men here. Of course, he proved that he had courage when he hopped out of the trench with that grenade and saved his company. I told you about it. But he has a quality, a kind of compassion for all men, that makes him tower above the rest of us. It is hard to take the measure of a man. There are so many bewildering standards. It's rather easier here.

Our use of the terms "here" and "there" is likely misleading. At this stage, as I have explained, we are not separated from you; I mean that we are not removed from the influences and conditions of the earth. I do not know how to search for expressions that will convey the truth simply to all who may read these letters. If we are going to get to the people with this, we must take some steps to interest a publisher. How would it do to see ——? Better think it over. I cannot advise. My judgment is no good.

We do not know when we are to be sent on to some other field. You remember we were once recalled when we had almost reached an important port of departure from this environment. The subject of these points of egress interests me greatly. It seems that there are certain defined avenues of intercommunication. We do not fly up and into some other sphere. We travel by established channels. I am very anxious to find out just what this means, and I shall hope to let you know. There must be some reason why, of all the millions who have passed the lines, no one has defined the boundaries of the unseen worlds. We talk the matter over, here, and have about agreed that language becomes inadequate, or we enter upon untranslatable conditions. Then, too, we may begin to count time by the thousand-year schedule. With the realization that you will soon be with us, we do not think to send you descriptions of what you are to see. One thing we must not lose sight of. This is the land of the living, and the loved ones are safe.

I picked up a kitten in my tent. An angel who was passing told me, quietly, to put it down. There was something curious in his look. I did not quite get it. You will be interested in this. But help me to keep our subject clear. It is easy to wander off into mazes of danger, although there is a perfectly straight, clean path to follow, if one will. I think it important for you to warn people of this danger. It is, I am told, particularly apparent in this zone. However, in any zone the soul carries its own means of defense.

Souls are being fused in these flames and purified. The bravery of men is applauded by the angels. I have seen them rush to welcome some little chap who has given his life to save others. That is the Christ quality — the highest form of love.

No human power can stop the war. The fighting may go on until the generations now on earth are all transferred to the spiritual worlds. God does not intervene. We cannot know His purposes. We only know that those who die yet live.

A lot of fellows in my tent were talking about the peculiar agony of suspense that mothers have to bear. Jack Wells spoke of that night in Gethsemane when the disciples slept. But somewhere in that garden was one who did not sleep. Mary watched all the dark night. Mothers are like that now.

There is no method about inter-space communication. The fuss of preparation is unnecessary and confusing. We do not need the material aids of paper and pencil, as our minds converse. I recommend the transcriptions because you are reporting these notes for a purpose. We want them as accurate as possible. Of course, I get balled up. But we'll keep sight of the plan.

The fight goes on ceaselessly. We do not share your feeling of appalling horror and pain. We see, rather, the hosts of clean young men coming to found their true democracy. Perhaps, you had better write "augment" in place of "found."

As we progress I find we are less inclined to criticize the efforts or condemn the failures of others. Something of truth must be in the minds of even the fakers who try to materialize spirits and set tables to jumping about a room. Primitive people were taught by means of crude spectacles. But now we have a way more suited to our developing intelligence.

I told you about my wireless work. It seems to us to indicate a change in the plan, a movement on the part of the Lord to intervene. We have all wondered why God did not sweep the Huns out of their wickedness. But humanity is, we suppose, allowed to exhaust itself before Divinity steps in. What are the words in the Book? Except the Lord stretch forth His hand, all flesh will perish from the earth. Please look up the exact wording.

Do not let us stop, now, to go over what I have said and correct inconsistencies. The way unrolls continually, and I get various angles of vision. I am not seeing much, as yet, that is so very different from the earth as you know it. I should say that the difference is chiefly in my new keenness of perception.

Wells makes occasional journeys to the place where his folks live. I quote him, particularly, because you know him. When I ask him how it is out yonder, he says for me to wait and see for myself. This may illustrate the point I have been trying to make. I asked him about the marriage of his older sister and her husband. I heard that the married become incorporated in one body. That is not just as it seemed at first to be. The two who love and marry are one in spirit and act and think as one soul. But they are separable in form and able to pursue their independent ways.

I have formed a friendship with Ann. She is as playful as a child, and I like her. But we are not mentally companionable. You remember a poem you liked by Miss Colson, about laughter in Heaven? Well, there is laughter here all right. I could not repeat a joke or any special thing that might be labeled humorous that is said or done. But there is a kind of joyousness that finds expression in laughter.

Cooper has gone back to Blighty. I missed him and asked Jack where he had gone. I do not understand yet. Will let you know. Am excited over news. Must go.

I have a delicate task here, mother. Cannot speak of it without higher authority. If I receive that, I know I can depend on your judgment and good taste. I have conferred with Wells, who is further advanced than I am. Wait alone for this.

There are lots of wireless men here, and we are busy. We are immensely improved in our work, and are able to decipher any code. The German operators cannot see us when we are around. But a man cannot be a wireless expert unless he has a finely developed sense. They feel us, all right. And they are afraid.

Mother, it is not a new thought, but it is true that all forms of life are created dual. We have spoken of the human and spiritual only briefly, because I am crassly ignorant, even yet. But Nature is also two-sided; material and ethereal. Everything is duplicated, forest, stream, landscape. Does that fact not make my place of residence more tangible to you? I should have told you sooner if I had heard of it.

Yes, I know what you are up against trying to get this across. Poor little mother! Her neighbors think she is a nut. But if you can get a few to try to write they will start things. Explain how simple it is. A place, a pencil, a pad of paper and a heart crying the name of a boy. That's all that is necessary.

I have permission to tell you that Cooper has, because of his understanding and compassion, been sent back home as an instructor. His body, sustained by some life principle which I cannot explain, has been all this time in a reconstruction hospital back of the French lines. You may see him with your own eyes. And you will know that any man who has crossed No Man's Land, and returned, has a message to the world from God.

Wells is hurrying on with his preparations to go. I do not know whether I am to go with him or not. I rather hope I may. And yet I do not want to cut off our line of communication. I think after I leave this environment, I shall have greater difficulty in communicating. As I have said before, I shall, perhaps, enter into less translatable conditions. The common speech may be inadequate. That, alone, may account for the futile messages transmitted through mediums. Still, the spirit is free to travel, and it is likely I may find a way to continue my letters to you and to give you such information as may be permitted.

You hope I will not go, dear? Well, I may hang around here indefinitely. Many are coming in, however, and it looks as though we might be transferred. One reason makes me rather keen to go. Jack told me about his younger sister last night. She is, it seems, a tremendous favorite with him. I said I wished I could see her. And there she was! A vision, really, in response to my wish. I don't believe heaven has a sweeter sight. I saw her plainly: dark-haired, blue-eyed, with a face of great brightness and fine color. Up to this time that I am relating the circumstances to you it has seemed miraculous, out of the natural order of things, that I could conjure up this girl's likeness. But I now realize that faculty to be the commonest in the world. You are exercising it, now, as you think of me and of her. Here is a point, mother. Maybe you can elaborate it. You project your thought to any scene or you draw toward you whatever vision you will. Words, one-syllabled or many, unlock the intelligences in all familiar ways. But the faculties of the creature made in God's own image are for the most part undeveloped, inert. Think of this in very simple terms. We are made in God's own image. Not faint resemblances of Him, but images. Look the word up in the best authorities.

We ought to be able to accomplish anything. At first I tried to say that the inner ear and the inner vision must be opened to make communication as easy as it is natural. Upon this, I am now sure, depend social relations of the worlds. We shall see each other, face to face, when we get rid of the acquired films that shut out vision, and the obstacles that impede the ways of sound.

A good deal of the old temper seems to be sticking to me. I got in with some Boches to-day on the battle field, and felt a rush of hate and fury, impossible to describe. I rushed among the wounded like a mad man. But He was there, ministering. I hardly know how I came away.

I talked with Wells about this, later, in my tent. He said we must give up thinking of Christ as ours alone. He quoted His words, as the mob howled around Him on Calvary:

"Father, forgive them, for they know not what they do."

It may be that the peculiar conditions of our work here make my judgments rather one-sided. I fancy in other locations,

America for instance, the people who have come out must see many things in altogether different lights. They are dying around you, every day. It should be perfectly simple to communicate with them. We are dwelling on the military exodus for the reasons we have outlined.

Mother, I often think of the days when I was a little boy. How good, and patient, you have always been to me. Don't forget in all this striving to let other hearts have comfort that the same old love is in your boy's heart for you.

I got your wire calling my attention to the scriptural statement that in heaven there is neither marriage or giving in marriage, and I do not know what to say. It seemed (until you gave me this jolt) that the Bible bears out everything that I have been able to tell you. Perhaps the chronicler got balled up in this particular quotation. For love and marriage are certainly in bud and flower here. I can see this fact with my own eyes. Many things that I write you I gather from others, relying on you to weed out that which does not contribute to the big plan, or any flagrant inconsistency that may rob some soul of a crumb of comfort. Don't bother about much else. This is a message, and it requires haste.

Of course, there are false reports and reporters here. Not makers of lies, so much, as natural dramatists who see all things in an exaggerated and spectacular form. Then, there are the symbolists who write the revelations.

Any critic would have me on the hip, and they will all be after you, if you can scare up a publisher to take this. And yet you will likely find a world more ready to listen, openly, to such a message than it has ever been before. Back in the human consciousness has always been a belief in spiritual things. The belief has been mixed with the terror of the unknown and denied because of that fear. Now the hand of God draws His worlds so near that they can whisper to each other.

Cooper will take up his old life on earth, and his mother will have her son. But he will not be the same. None of those who go back will be the same. Angels, dressed in stained and faded khaki, will walk the familiar streets. Listen to them.

Dogs come and go freely, back and forth across the invisible line. I am told this as a fact. They do not need to leave their natural bodies to associate with those who have died. They often follow their masters. Other animals have not quite these privileges, but after dissolution they appear here. I may not be clear. I often find a certain embarrassment in saying things that I, myself, would once have called bunk. But I guess they are true, all right.

Try and remember, mother, dear, that I do not know much more than I did when I left you. That is, no wisdom has been given me. I am, however, quickened in my perceptions, and my natural bent is encouraged. I have every opportunity to learn. I suppose arbitrary rules must underlie this harmonious system of living. But they are not felt. None of us are fretted by "shalt nots" or "shalls." We seem to go along about as we please. But we please to move with enthusiastic energy; if we did not, I suppose we might feel the sharp stick.

We do not have classes in the ordinary acceptance of the term. But men of like interests gather and exchange information. I have learned a lot about wireless that I hope to communicate some other time; through a technician, maybe.

I want to suggest to you to keep these notes entirely apart from anything else I write you. Do not make a big book. Let it be only a few pages to hide in a mourner's sleeve. Call it a sleeve book, if you want to. I think that might convey an idea. But in any case keep it free from subjects or speculations outside the main plan, which is: comfort for war-robbed humanity. Keep after that! There is no death! and don't let any attractive theory sidetrack you. The firing is continual and terrific. I must get on the job of guiding the boys through. They will come without fear.

You feel the need for more definite information about this existence before you go out to talk of immortality. But you have all that your untutored Bob can tell you, and a thousandfold more in John. Read the fourteenth chapter again. It is all there: the whole plan of eternal life, continuous life, I mean. There are no mansions here, that I see. But, as I have explained, we form one of many special brigades or divisions of soldiers, and are now in active relief service in the war zone. We have tents and equipment; we talk and walk and choose our companions. We love or like, or avoid others, according to our own impulses. We look as we did in the flesh. It seems almost as though we had only slipped out of our skins, as the snakes do. A natural process, familiar to simple people, but too simple to be considered by those butterfly hunters that try to net the soul. Please cut that out, mother. You might leave the comparison to the snake, however; I think that holds some truth.

The premise is all right, isn't it? You have it clear? There is no death. Life goes on without handicap or hindrance. We are very busy. There is no talk of peace, here. I gather from what the angels say that the war will go until many more of the valiant have come through this valley, and have gone on to form a new democracy on another plane. I am reporting impressions, and have no authority for my conclusions, except the authority of my own intelligence. Do not be terrorized even should an invasion of America be made. The easiest thing in life is death.

Jack Wells and I are very close friends. His sister's name is Alice, and she has grown up in the country beyond, where his folks live. It seems all reach or return to maturity. Youth blossoms and flowers, but does not decay. I can call up her vision at any time. But I want her near.

Christ walks among the wounded continually. The dying see Him, and the hurt are healed by His hand. Many have told me, and several times I have felt Him near. Once, for a moment, I saw Him, I told you.

Preserve an unemotional mind, dear. Sanity and simplicity are essential to our purpose. Do not go on any tangent of description, or undertake analyses. What is here is here. Some people will find what we have hoped to give them. Others must find comfort in different ways.

You have understood, haven't you? That I no longer stop and dictate these things to you? I talk to you as I perform my tasks, or lie at rest, or march along my ways. It is almost certain that we are to be ordered on within a few hours' time. Destination unknown. But wherever it may be, I shall travel with eager curiosity. I shall surely tell you all I can. It may be that one returns to this boundary for purposes of communication. That will develop later.

Take care of your health. You have a task that you must not fail to accomplish. You can bind up some of the most grievous wounds in the world. Keep your strength and go up and down the wailing places on the earth, and say and know: "Thy son liveth." That's your part.

Isn't it foolish to try to convince any one of anything? What words are there to prove or disprove that life was and is and ever shall be? If one does not realize now naturally and without argument that he is an undying soul, he will come to realize it some time. Why hurry him?

I am on the march. And I am thinking of you, and the eternal verities, and of the wondering of a boy walking beside me, and of the land that lies beyond our Jordan. And through and over all these other thoughts is something that permeates them with a kind of thrilling fragrance. It is love, I think, mother.

We are passing through a land laid waste and yet triumphant. I felt immensely surprised to see in all its beauty one great cathedral that had been destroyed. The angel said that all such buildings of prayer and song are spiritual and beyond vandal desecration. The bricks will be restored to conform to the imperishable idea. I do not want to get metaphysical (in the bewildering way). I just want to say that I am improving in spiritual vision. When we started out before, you remember, I was only able to see the obvious: broken bodies of flesh and of stone. To-day I see the immortal structures.

It is so simple, dear. Here I am on the open road that all humanity travels, going toward the enlarged opportunities that await me. I have been talking to the boy. He is not more than fourteen. But he fought his fight. Spenser has taken him under his wing. I don't mean that literally.

None of us have wings. But that reminds me of what I was going to tell you about the messengers. Some way those old Greeks must have been in touch with this side of the world. Olympus must have pierced the invisible. For instance, these messengers wear little wings on their feet. I do not know whether they grow there or not. One passed us a moment ago, treading the air with incredible grace. Hermes reborn. They are employed between some higher command and our own.

' Spenser is reconciled to wait for his girl to join him. There is so much to do that the time passes with much swiftness in and out of light and dark. We have·the same natural divisions that you have. Why should this not be true? We are still on earth. As we pass, differences may arise that we are not conscious of, but so far as I am able I shall keep you informed.

We have now reached a river of surpassing beauty. I have always felt, and I am more impressed than ever with the feeling now, that a river is more spiritual than any other expression of physical nature. It may be that this is our port of egress. It is. We have been commanded to halt. One desire seems to animate us all: that is to run down and swim in this shining stream. We have thrown away our outer garments and are plunging in. Good-by for now. I am running down to the water as I used to run down to the old mill-stream, tingling with joy. . . .

ImTheStory.com

Personalized Classic Books in many genre's

Unique gift for kids, partners, friends, colleagues

Customize:

- Character Names
- Upload your own front/back cover images (optional)
- Inscribe a personal message/dedication on the inside page (optional)

Customize many titles Including
- Alice in Wonderland
- Romeo and Juliet
- The Wizard of Oz
- A Christmas Carol
- Dracula
- Dr. Jekyll & Mr. Hyde
- And more...

Emily's Adventures in Wonderland

Ryan & Julia